5.7

W9-AYR-714

Hurricane Katrina
Strikes the Gulf Coast

Disaster & Survival

Mara Miller

Enslow Publishers, Inc.

40 Industrial Road   PO Box 38
Box 398   Aldershot
Berkeley Heights, NJ 07922 Hants GU12 6BP
USA   UK
http://www.enslow.com

To the victims of Hurricane Katrina
May they find strength in the community of our nation

Library of Congress Cataloging-in-Publication Data

Miller, Mara, 1968–
    Hurricane Katrina strikes the Gulf Coast : disaster & survival / Mara Miller.
        p. cm. — (Deadly disasters)
    Includes bibliographical references and index.
    ISBN-10: 0-7660-2803-8
    1. Hurricane Katrina, 2005—Juvenile literature. 2. Hurricanes—Juvenile literature. 3. Disaster victims—United States—Juvenile literature. 4. Rescue work—United States—Juvenile literature. I. Title. II. Series.
    QC945.M54 2006
    363.34'922—dc22

                                                    2005030989

ISBN-13: 978-0-7660-2803-6

Printed in the United States of America

10 9 8 7 6 5 4 3 2

To Our Readers: We have done our best to make sure all Internet Addresses in this book were active and appropriate when we went to press. However, the author and the publisher have no control over and assume no liability for the material available on those Internet sites or on other Web sites they may link to. Any comments or suggestions can be sent by e-mail to comments@enslow.com or to the address on the back cover.

Illustration Credits: AP/Wide World Photos, pp. 1, 4, 6, 9, 13, 18, 20, 22, 24, 25, 27, 28, 30, 32, 34, 35, 37, 39; Enslow Publishers, Inc., p. 15.

Cover Illustration: AP/Wide World Photos

Contents

The winds of Hurricane Katrina bend palm trees in the Grande Lagoon area of Pensacola, Florida.

CHAPTER 1

Katrina Gains Strength

THERE WAS NOT MUCH TIME TO WARN FLORIDA. A major storm was coming. A group of dark clouds and rain, called Tropical Depression 12, had developed rapidly over the Bahamas—islands only fifty miles from Florida's coast. Rain pelted the tiny islands. Palm trees bowed in the wind. Winds reached 40 miles per hour (mph). The National Weather Service upgraded Tropical Depression 12 to a tropical storm. They gave the storm a name—Katrina.[1]

Florida officials had to hurry to warn the public and ready emergency crews. If the storm stalled, fifteen inches of rain could fall. "People need to take this storm seriously," said Florida Governor Jeb Bush. "It is a major storm that could create flooding."[2]

Some Florida residents prepared, but others did not. "I don't think anybody is really terribly concerned about this one because it looks like it's going to be a tropical storm," said Jean Dowling, vice president of a Florida residents' association.[3]

"This is a Nightmare"

On the morning of August 26, 2005, Katrina whipped through the Miami area, snapping trees and power lines. The National Weather Service clocked wind speeds of 87 miles per hour. Katrina was a level 1 hurricane. The storm was stronger than many people expected. Siding came off houses, and wind scattered debris. Sheets of rain flooded the streets.

"It was like something out of a movie," said Amanda Sullivan, who stayed in her home during the storm. "There

were metal pipes flying off the building, and a 20-foot trailer came flying through here."[4]

"This was a one, a Category 1," said

This family's street was flooded after Hurricane Katrina tore through Florida City, Florida.

Hal Gunnison, staring at a huge mass of tangled twisted branches and roots covering the street outside his home. "This is a nightmare."[5]

Katrina left 1.2 million people in and around Florida without power and caused $600 million in damage.[6] Eleven people died in Florida as a result of the storm.

Katrina spun into the Gulf of Mexico. There, the storm grew more powerful. "I don't remember seeing conditions as favorable as this for a strengthening hurricane for a long time," said National Hurricane Center director Max Mayfield.[7]

Katrina Targets New Orleans

Katrina was a dangerous storm and was headed straight for New Orleans. The city is at a particular risk for flooding. It lies below sea level and is surrounded on three sides by water. Lake Pontchartrain is to the north. The Mississippi River flows south of the city. The Gulf of Mexico lies to the east and south. Levees built around the city help keep out water. But a Category 4 or 5 hurricane could flow over or break the levees.

"The worst case is a hurricane moving in from due south of the city," said Joseph Suhayda in June 2002. At the time, he developed a computer model of what could happen to New Orleans during a Category 4 or 5 hurricane. He predicted that waves of water called storm surges could wash over the levees.[8]

"Another scenario is that some part of the levee would fail," Suhayda said. "[If the] levees broke, the break will get wider and wider. The water will flow through the city and stop only when it reaches the next higher thing."[9] If that happened, New Orleans would fill up like a bathtub. Any levees that remained intact would hold the water in the city and not allow it to flow back out.

On Sunday, August 28, C. Ray Nagin, the mayor of New Orleans, ordered everyone to leave the city. "We are facing a storm that most of us have long feared. The storm surge will most likely topple our levee system."[10]

But thousands of New Orleans residents did not have cars or could not afford to take a plane, train, or bus out of the city. More than nine thousand people flocked to the Superdome arena. The Superdome was set up by the city as the shelter of last resort. It was a place for people who had nowhere else to go. Some people stayed home despite the warnings.

The Unthinkable: A Category 5

Katrina also threatened other cities. Authorities in Gulfport, Mississippi, turned about a dozen schools and public buildings into shelters. However, the buildings were not made to withstand the 140 to 150 mph winds

People who were unable to evacuate New Orleans gather at the city's Superdome on August 28, 2005.

that Katrina could bring. "We're asking people to get out of the area," said Joe Spraggins, the director of emergency operations for Harrison County, Mississippi, "and to get out fast."[11]

On Sunday night, Katrina grew into a Category 5 hurricane. Winds reached 175 mph. By 10:00 P.M., Katrina's eye was about 170 miles south-southeast of New Orleans. The storm was moving north-northwest at about 10 to 15 mph. It would hit land early in the morning.[12]

What Is a Hurricane?

HURRICANES ARE VIOLENT STORMS THAT FORM IN the tropics. They have sustained wind speeds of at least 74 mph. Hurricanes are classified by the Saffir-Simpson Hurricane Scale.[1] Categories from 1 to 5 rank the strength of the winds and describe the damage that can be expected from the different wind speeds. Categories 3, 4, and 5 are considered major hurricanes. They are likely to do a lot of damage.[2]

The Gulf of Mexico: Hurricane Hotspot

The Gulf of Mexico was warmer than usual when Katrina entered. It was as warm as bath water. A hurricane can be thought of as a heat engine.[3] It uses warm water for fuel. The warm ocean surface heats and moistens the air over the water. This warm, moist air rises into the hurricane.

Saffir-Simpson Scale

Category	Sustained Winds	Damage	Example Storms
1	74–95 mph	Minimal: Damage to plants and trees, and unanchored mobile homes. No real structural damage.	Hurricane Irene, 1999
2	96–110	Moderate: Some trees blown down. Major damage to exposed mobile homes. Some damage to roofs, windows, and doors.	Hurricane Floyd, 1999 Hurricane Frances, 2004
3	111–130	Extensive: Large trees blown down. Mobile homes destroyed. Some damage to roofs of buildings. Some structural damage to small buildings.	Hurricane Ivan, 2004 Hurricane Rita, 2005
4	131–155	Extreme: Large trees blown down. Complete destruction of mobile homes. Extensive damage to roofs, windows, and doors. Roofs destroyed on many small homes.	Hurricane Charley, 2004 Hurricane Katrina, 2005
5	>155	Catastrophic: Roofs destroyed on many homes and industrial buildings. Extensive damage to windows and doors. Some buildings completely destroyed.[4]	Hurricane Camille, 1969 Hurricane Andrew, 1992

The water in the air cools as it rises and condenses into droplets. In this process, heat is released. The released heat is energy, which fuels the high winds of the storm.

Also, in the Gulf of Mexico, there was very little wind shear. Wind shear is the difference between the wind's speed or direction at the surface and the wind's speed or direction high in the atmosphere. Big differences in wind speed or direction can knock over the thunderstorm and weaken the hurricane. The especially warm water and low wind shear made conditions perfect for Katrina to become a monster.

Naming a Hurricane

The general term for a hurricane is tropical cyclone. Tropical cyclones form from clusters of thunderstorms—called tropical depressions—that have started to spin. North of the equator, tropical cyclones spin counterclockwise. South of the equator, the storms spin clockwise. In the Atlantic Ocean, Gulf of Mexico, and Eastern Pacific, tropical cyclones are called hurricanes. In the Western Pacific, they are called typhoons. In the Indian Ocean, this type of storm is simply called a cyclone.

The National Weather Service upgrades a tropical depression to a tropical storm when sustained wind speeds exceed 40 mph. At this point the storm is given a name. In 1979, a committee developed a six-year rotating list of names for storms. When a storm causes major damage the name is removed and a replacement is chosen by committee.[5]

Hurricane Katrina was the eleventh named storm to form during the 2005 hurricane season. The hurricane season starts June 1 and lasts until November 30. August and September have the most hurricane activity.

High Winds

Hurricanes spin around a cloudless, circular area in the center of the storm. This is called the eye. In the eye, the winds are light and the sky is clear. The eye of a hurricane usually spans from 20 to 30 miles in diameter. Sometimes people will go outside during the eye of the storm thinking that a hurricane has passed. This can be dangerous when the winds pick up again.

The eye wall surrounds the eye. It is made of dense clouds and has some of the strongest winds. Katrina's eye wall had wind gusts of over 200 mph when it was over the warmest water in the Gulf of Mexico.[6] There is a lot

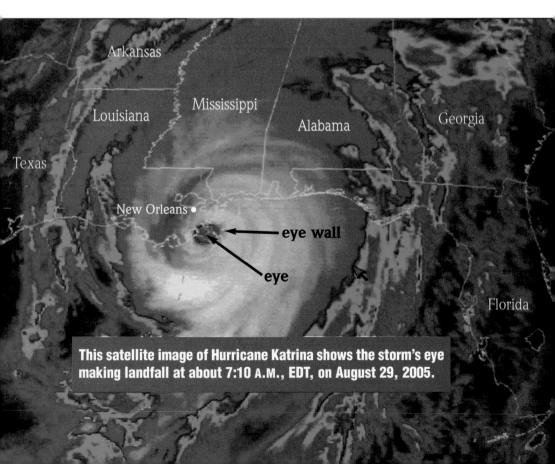

This satellite image of Hurricane Katrina shows the storm's eye making landfall at about 7:10 A.M., EDT, on August 29, 2005.

of wind damage around the eye of the storm. But the damage on the right side of the hurricane's path, or track, is likely to be greater than the damage to the left. (For example, if a hurricane was moving north, the damage to the east would be greater than the damage to the west.)

Floods and Tornadoes

Another danger during a hurricane is a storm surge. A storm surge is water that is pushed over the shoreline by the high winds. The surge can act like a bulldozer and clear away cars, houses, and anything else in its path.

Storm surge was a huge concern as Katrina headed for New Orleans. The National Hurricane Center predicted storm surges of up to 28 feet.[7] A storm surge of that height would flow over the city's levees.

There is still a lot of water in the air after a hurricane strikes. The resulting rains can drench cities with more than 20 inches of water. Floods account for over half of all hurricane deaths. Even six inches of fast-moving flood-water can sweep a person off his or her feet.[8]

Hurricanes lose power fairly quickly after they hit land. Without the warm water, their source of energy is gone. But the threat continues even as the winds die down. About 70 percent of hurricanes will spawn at least one tornado. The funnel-shaped clouds can touch down even three days after a hurricane makes landfall. But most tornadoes occur in the first day or two.[9]

Calculating the Strike Zone

As Katrina made its way toward land, forecasters tried to predict where it would strike. Hurricane hunters are

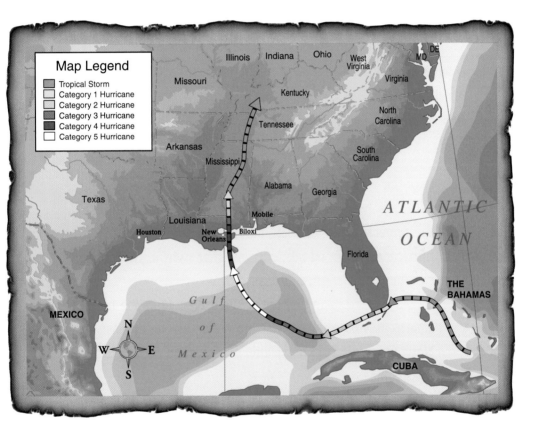

After hitting Florida, Katrina quickly strengthened over the warm waters of the Gulf of Mexico before it rammed into the Gulf Coast.

scientists who gather information by flying into hurricanes. They drop weather-sensing canisters with parachutes, called dropsondes, into the storm. The dropsondes measure humidity, air pressure, temperature, and wind speed. The hurricane hunters also fly around the hurricane to see how big it is and measure the eye of the storm. Other information is gathered from satellite images. Satellites take pictures of hurricanes from outer space.

Storm surge was a huge concern as Katrina headed for New Orleans.

A computer uses this information to predict the future movement and intensity of the hurricane. But even with all this information, the path of a hurricane is hard to predict. Steering winds in the upper atmosphere can change and alter the path of a hurricane. Warm eddies, currents that swirl in the water, can increase a storm's intensity.

As Katrina neared shore, a slight change in the hurricane's movement sent Katrina's eye 50 miles east of New Orleans. The hurricane was headed straight into Mississippi.

CHAPTER

3

Katrina Strikes

KATRINA PLOWED INTO THE CITIES OF BILOXI AND Gulfport, Mississippi on the morning of August 29, 2005. It was a Category 4 hurricane. Winds raged at 165 mph. The storm surge reached 22 feet. Some people risked their lives to videotape the storm. They filmed 4 feet of water rushing into the front lobby of a hotel. A driverless car rammed into the front door. The fast-moving water had carried it there.[1]

Outside, trees bent and snapped. The wind roared like a freight train. Parking lots looked like seas with ocean-sized waves. One man found an 800-pound seal in his front yard.[2] Edwina Craft rode out the terrifying storm at the Biloxi Regional Medical Center. "The room was shaking. The windows were shaking," she said. "They moved

Alex Curtis, age twelve, sits amid the damage in Biloxi, Mississippi, the day after Hurricane Katrina hit. His family lost the roof of their home in the storm.

us from the sixth floor to the bottom floor . . . It flooded down there, and then the lights went off."[3]

Timothy Wagner weathered the hurricane in an empty commercial building in Gulfport. That was after the walls of his brick apartment building buckled and collapsed. "When everything started crumbling, I was dodging cinder-blocks," he said.[4]

David and Kay Andre crawled into their attic as their home flooded. Then the wind began blowing holes in their roof. "A gust would come and we'd pray the house would hold," said Kay Andre.[5]

"The water got higher and higher," said Joy Schovest. She tried to ride out the storm in her apartment. "[The surge] pushed all the doors open and we swam out. It was terrifying. You should have seen the cars floating around us"[6]

The Aftermath in Mississippi and Alabama

In Long Beach, Mississippi, the storm surge had been so strong that it lifted apartment buildings off their foundations and washed them away. The only thing left was concrete and a car in the middle of the swimming pool.

Piles of shrimp boats, cars, and splintered wood littered the streets. Gulfport Fire Chief Pat Sullivan looked at the damage and said, "Complete devastation . . . We've got boats that have gone into buildings."[7]

A fire burns near the former site of an apartment complex in Long Beach, Mississippi, on August 31, 2005.

After the storm, the Coast Guard tried to rescue those who remained. "People are still trapped in attics and on second floors of their homes," said Biloxi spokesman Vincent Creel. Rescuers dangled from helicopters. They plucked survivors off their roofs. But not everyone survived. "We are discovering bodies, and the numbers will continue to rise," said Creel.[8]

Hurricane Katrina spanned three states. In Alabama, four hundred thousand people and businesses lost power.[9] An oil rig broke free during the high winds. It wedged under a bridge near Mobile and forced it to close. In addition, thirty-six tornadoes spun off Hurricane Katrina in a number of states.

The Winds in New Orleans

In New Orleans, Louisiana, strong winds and heavy rain hammered the city for eight hours. The 145-mph winds blew out windows, downed power lines, and felled trees. Boats crashed into shore. A levee failed in the Bernard Parish neighborhood. Muddy water swirled down the narrow streets. Sections of a 5.4-mile-long bridge that crossed Lake Pontchartrain collapsed.

Thousands of evacuees huddled in the New Orleans Superdome. As the storm blew through, the wind ripped two holes in the sports arena's domed roof. Water leaked in around the elevators, stairwells, and through the 15-foot-long tears.

"I could have stayed at home and watched my roof blow off," said Harald Johnson, "Instead, I came down here and watched the Superdome roof blow off. It's no big deal; getting wet is not like dying."[10]

The electricity in the arena went out around 5:00 A.M. Generators powered some lights, but not the air-conditioning. The crowded Superdome became hot and muggy.

After Katrina passed, it seemed that New Orleans had

Light pours through the holes in the Superdome's roof caused by Katrina. The playing field was littered with trash because survivors of the storm had stayed in the stadium for days.

survived. The winds had been intense. But it looked like most of the city avoided the devastating floods.

However, water was spilling in through a hole in the 17th Street Canal levee. Those who were nearby could see Lake Pontchartrain flowing into the city like a waterfall. But they could not spread the news. Phone lines were down. Power was out. Winds had destroyed the cellular-phone towers.

Water was quickly filling the city of New Orleans. And there was no way to warn people.

CHAPTER

4

New Orleans Floods

THROUGHOUT THE NEXT DAY, THE WATER KEPT RISING in New Orleans. The hole in the 17th Street Canal levee grew until it was two city blocks wide.[1] Attempts to fix the levee failed. Soon, 80 percent of New Orleans was underwater. In some places, the water reached the rooftops of houses.[2]

Sam Marconi was grilling a hamburger when it began to flood. "The next minute there was four feet of water covering the top of my grill," he said. People scrambled to reach higher ground. "I saw dozens of people breaking out of the attic with their axes."[3]

In Need of Rescue

Brian Kornsey began rescuing people at 10:00 P.M. on Monday night. He paddled his flatboat through the

Water pours through a break in a levee along the Inner Harbor Navigation Canal in New Orleans on August 30, 2005.

streets. The neighborhoods had no power. It was pitch black. "We didn't have no flashlights," Kornsey said. "I saw three dead people floating near Claiborne Street."[4]

Problems with communication slowed rescue attempts. Only a few cell phones could get through. Chris Robinson managed to talk to the Associated Press. "The water's rising pretty fast," he said. "I got a hammer and an ax and a crowbar. But I'm holding off on breaking through the roof until the last minute. Tell someone to come get me please. I want to live."[5]

Thousands of people were rescued by boat or by air. Firefighters brought more than eight hundred residents to the top of a highway overpass. But there was not enough food or water for them. "That was the worst part because these people were looking to us for answers," said Darrin Cagnalotti, a captain in the fire department. "Our job was to get them away from the water, which was the biggest hazard, but the whole situation was extremely frustrating for us."[6]

Trouble at the Superdome

Rescuers also brought people to the Superdome. Soon, more than fifteen thousand people hoped to find food,

Crews from the Bay St. Louis Emergency Management Agency rescue the Taylor family from the top of their SUV as floodwaters rage around them.

water, and shelter in the sports arena. But officials had not planned for the arena to hold that many people. And they had not planned for the amount of time people needed to stay. Food and water was limited.

"We could never get more supplies through, I don't know why," said National Guard officer Lieutenant Colonel Gary Nunn. "[W]e had to start rationing the food early. [We gave] people only one meal packet and a bottle of water twice a day."[7] Food lines were two hours long. Survivors shoved and pushed in the line. Exhausted elderly people were often unable to keep their places.

The Superdome had other problems, too. It had limited power. The heat was intense. The smell was worse. By Wednesday, the city's water gave out. Toilets overflowed and were useless. "We pee on the floor. We are like animals," said evacuee Taffany Smith.[8] Michael Clark, another evacuee, explained, "[People] were [going to the bathroom] into the sinks and garbage cans and behind the concession stands. You got it all over your shoes. You were tracking it all over the place."[9]

Evacuees had no place to get clean either. Most did not even have a change of clothes. Some sick and elderly people died while waiting for relief.

People wanted to leave the hot, stinky dome, but they were trapped. One man leaped a barricade. National Guard Sergeant Caleb Wells chased him down. "He didn't realize how bad things [were] out there," said Wells. "We took him to the terrace and said: 'Look.'" When the man saw the rising floodwater, "he just broke down. He started bawling. We took him back inside."[10]

Forgotten at the Convention Center

Another fifteen thousand to twenty thousand people gathered at the New Orleans Convention Center. Some were directed there by the police. The convention center was

Terri Jones comforts and tries to cool down an overheated fellow survivor at the Convention Center in New Orleans on September 1, 2005.

27

half a mile away from the Superdome. The conditions inside were even worse.

Officials never planned to use the convention center as a shelter. There was not enough food and water. No one screened those who entered for weapons. Several reports of violence increased feelings of fear.

The evacuees felt forgotten. Reporters described the terrible conditions in the news. But in an interview, Federal Emergency Management Agency (FEMA) director Michael Brown said he was unaware of the crowds at the convention center until September 2.[11] Later, he said he was actually aware of the problems at the convention center a day earlier.

Some people walked across the Crescent City Connection Bridge to Gretna, Louisiana, a suburb of New Orleans. When they got there,

FEMA Director Michael Brown held a press conference on September 4, 2005. There, he introduced Lieutenant-general Russell Honore of the Air Force, who headed rescue and security operations in New Orleans.

police told the evacuees that they could not enter. "We walked, probably 200 people, about a two-hour trek," said evacuee Tim Sheer. "We got to the top of the bridge. They stopped us with shotguns."[12]

Lawlessness and Fear

In New Orleans, people began breaking the law. Gunshots rang out in the streets. Looters carried off goods from stores wrecked by the hurricane. Some people only took food, water, and the supplies that they needed to live. Others carried off jewelry, televisions, vacuum cleaners, and other expensive items.

Lack of reliable communication and limited leadership gave rise to rumors and fear. Newspapers reported gangs, murders, rapes, and sniper fire. Some reports may not have been accurate, but others were all too real.

Respiratory therapist Blake Bergeron was trying to evacuate very sick patients from Charity Hospital. He heard two or three bullets zip into the floodwaters. "The soldiers shouted for us to get down," he said.[13]

At first, the police were instructed to save lives. But as disorder grew, the police returned to patrol duty. National Guard troops also came to restore order. "These troops know how to shoot and kill," said Louisiana Governor Kathleen Blanco, trying to regain control of the city.[14]

"An Engineering Nightmare"

The Army Corps of Engineers had other problems. They had to repair the levees, which were now underwater. "The challenge is an engineering nightmare," said Governor Kathleen Blanco.[15]

Engineers filled 3,000-pound cargo containers with sand, rock, and other heavy materials. They carried these containers and 180 concrete barriers by helicopter and placed them into the breach.

Eventually, huge city pumps started to remove the water. A single pumping station could remove 75,000 gallons of water per second.[16] But it was not clear how many pumps were working. Many people wondered when they would be able to return to their homes and what they would find when the water was gone.

Soldiers unload supplies in New Orleans on September 4, 2005. They were assigned to patrol the streets to stop the lawlessness that arose after the city flooded.

After Katrina

I T TOOK SIX DAYS TO EVACUATE ALL THE PEOPLE FROM the Superdome and the New Orleans Convention Center. Many evacuees boarded buses bound for Texas. They would stay in the Houston Astrodome until they found a better place to live.

It was a relief to leave New Orleans. But the future was still uncertain. Ervin Doyle arrived at the Astrodome with his two small sons. "I do not even know where my wife and two daughters are," said Doyle. "I just want to get a little help getting established, so I can get my life back together and go back home—but that's if I want to go back."[1]

The Poor Could Not Leave

Many of the people who did not leave before the hurricane were poor or elderly. Some did not have cars or enough money to pay for bus fare. Others had medical problems

Milvertha Hendricks, age eighty-seven, uses a blanket designed to look like the American flag to shield herself from the rain at the city's Convention Center on September 1, 2005.

that made leaving difficult. These people had not been considered in the city's evacuation plans. Hurricane Katrina also exposed a deep poverty felt by many minorities in New Orleans. Representative Elijah Cummings of Maryland declared, "We cannot allow . . . the difference between those who lived and those who died" to be "nothing more than poverty, age or skin color."[2]

Assessing the Many Mistakes

Many mistakes were made before, during, and after the hurricane. Predictions were ignored. Evacuation plans failed. And help did not come fast enough. David Vitter, a senator from Louisiana, gave the federal government an F for its handling of the storm's aftermath.[3] Aaron Broussard, a New Orleans's parish president, criticized FEMA. "We had Wal-Mart deliver three trailer trucks of water . . .

FEMA turned them back," he said in a TV interview.[4] FEMA director Michael Brown resigned from his job because of criticism. But people were not only upset with FEMA. They were angry at every level of government—from the president down to governor and mayor.

Nursing Homes and Hospitals

The sick and elderly suffered during Hurricane Katrina. In one nursing home, the elderly were simply abandoned without care. Thirty-four people died as a result.[5] The two owners were arrested and charged with negligent homicide (a charge brought against people whose irresponsible acts or inaction caused people in their care to die). More than 215 of the 1,048 dead in New Orleans were found in and around hospitals and nursing homes.[6] Six hospitals and thirteen nursing homes in Louisiana are under investigation for their treatment of the people in their care.[7]

Harsh Conditions and a New Threat

People wanted to return to their houses to see the damage. They wanted to see if anything could be saved. On September 26, Mayor Nagin announced a plan to let people back into the less-damaged areas of New Orleans. Federal officials thought it was too soon. They said it was unsafe. "There are issues about lack of potable [drinkable] water; there are basic services that are not in place;

we are still trying to constitute [set up] a 911 service," said Thad Allen, the vice admiral in charge of the federal recovery.[8]

But a bigger threat convinced people to leave the city for a second time. Another hurricane, Rita, had formed in the Gulf of Mexico. It was a Category 5 hurricane and about two days away from shore. Rita was headed for Houston, Texas, instead of New Orleans. However, Louisiana was on the right side of the storm's track. The levees in New Orleans were weak and could burst again.

All of Houston evacuated. Those who had left the Superdome for the Astrodome were evacuated again. "It looks like the storm is following me," said Katrina survivor Wayne Sylvester.[9]

The crowds of people leaving created backups on the highway up to 100 miles long. People sat in traffic jams for more than ten hours.

Bodies of hurricane and flood victims could be seen all over New Orleans after Hurricane Katrina. This body was covered with a sheet by a loved one, making a temporary grave.

Soldiers responded more quickly to Hurricane Rita than they did to Katrina.

Cars ran out of gas on the highway. "We've been going 12 hours," said Madra Moore, trying to get out of Houston, "and we're going nowhere fast. The police have got everything blocked off. We just got to sit here."[10]

Rita was a Category 3 when it struck land near the Texas-Louisiana border. High winds pushed water over the repaired levees. Parts of New Orleans flooded for a second time. "New Orleans is . . . back to square one: pump, pump, pump and start over again," said Ivor van Heerden, the deputy director of the Louisiana State University Hurricane Center.[11]

But this time, most everyone had left the area before the storm hit. Some lessons had already been learned from Katrina's aftermath.

6

The Next Hurricane

SOME SCIENTISTS WORRY THAT HURRICANES ARE becoming more frequent and stronger because of global warming. Global warming is an increase in the earth's temperature, including its sea-surface temperature. Since warmer water gives hurricanes more energy, the increase in sea-surface temperature could make hurricane seasons worse. The year 2005 was one of the worst hurricane seasons on record.

Other scientists think that the recent increase in hurricane-season intensity has little to do with global warming. They think that Rita followed so closely after Katrina because the Atlantic is in a normal period of increased hurricane activity.

Evacuation Plans

States on the Atlantic and Gulf coasts plan how to handle a hurricane. Some of the plans for Hurricane Katrina worked well. New Orleans's system for getting drivers out of the city quickly without huge traffic jams worked. Other things went very badly. Over 1,250 people died during Hurricane Katrina and its floods.[1]

After Katrina, officials took steps to avoid making the same mistakes twice. When Hurricane Rita threatened, hundreds of buses were on hand to help people get out of Houston. Tons of food and water were made ready for an emergency. Twenty-six helicopters and five teams with high-tech communications gear got into position.

"We are determined to learn the lessons of Katrina, and that's why we have been assessing what's been

The American Red Cross prepared this shelter for victims of Hurricane Rita at the First Baptist Church in Tyler, Texas.

working and what hasn't been working and taking steps to address those issues," said White House spokesman Scott McClellan.[2]

"I think they have come to their senses," said Richard Krimm, a former FEMA agent. "If they had done for Hurricane Katrina what they are doing [for Hurricane Rita], you wouldn't have had the debacle in New Orleans."[3]

Planning at Home

Just like the government, individuals in places threatened by hurricanes need to have a plan. Everyone should know what the risks are for the area in which he or she lives. If a person is asked to evacuate, he or she should do so quickly. People who are not asked to evacuate during a hurricane should go to a local shelter, another safe place in their community, or the safest room in their house.

People living in a hurricane area should prepare a disaster supply kit. This kit should include water, food, blankets, a flashlight, batteries, clothing, a first aid kit, money, important documents, toiletries, keys, tools, and a weather radio.[4] The kit should be portable, so it can be taken in a car or on foot. People should also fill up their cars with gas if they know a hurricane is coming.

During Hurricane Katrina, many families were separated. Relatives inside and outside of New Orleans did not

Hurricane survivor Christine Felder hugs her son John after they are reunited on September 9, 2005. The two of them were separated when they were evacuated to two different cities.

know how to find their loved ones. Another part of a hurricane plan is to have an out-of-state friend or relative as a family contact. That way everyone will know whom to call with news.

"There Was Bravery and Kindness"

Hurricane Katrina brought out the best and the worst in people. Most Americans hope that the effects of the storm will make the United States stronger as a nation and more prepared for the next disaster that strikes.

"We helped in what little way we could," said a police officer, who later collapsed from exhaustion and had to be hospitalized. "I saw terrible things. Just terrible things. But I also saw people sharing what little food they had. There was bravery and kindness."[5]

Deadliest Hurricanes in the United States

Rank	Location/Name	Year	Category	Death Toll
1	Galveston, Texas	1900	4	8,000–12,000
2	Lake Okeechobee, Florida	1928	4	2,500–3,000
3	Hurricane Katrina: The Gulf Coast	2005	4	1,281*
4	Cheniere Caminanda, Louisiana	1893	4	1,100–1,400
5	Sea Islands in Georgia and South Carolina	1893	3	1,000–2,000
6	Georgia and South Carolina	1881	2	700
7 (tie)	Florida Keys, Louisiana, and Southern Texas	1935	5	600
7 (tie)	New England	1938	3	600
8	Florida Keys	1935	5	408
9	Last Island, Louisiana	1856	4	400

*As of December 2005

Sources: "Table 2. Mainland U.S. tropical cyclones causing 25 or greater deaths 1851–2004," *NOAA*, 2004, <http://www.nhc.noaa.gov/gifs/table2.gif> (November 11, 2005).

"Post-Tropical Cyclone Report for Hurricane Katrina," *National Weather Service Forecasting Office*, November 9, 2005, <http://www.srh.noaa.gov/lix/html/psh_katrina.htm> (November 13, 2005).

Chapter Notes

Chapter 1. Katrina Gains Strength

1. Tim O'Meilia, "Surprise Evolved as Depression Fueled Wave," *Palm Beach Post*, August 25, 2005, p. 1A.

2. Graham Brink, Joni James, and Tamara Lush, "Katrina Washes In, Early and Ornery," *St. Petersburg Times*, August 26, 2005, p. 1A.

3. John Pain, "Florida Largely Undeterred as Katrina Nears," *Journal-Gazette*, August 25, 2005, p. 7A.

4. Joseph B. Treaster, "Hurricane Drenches Florida and Leaves Seven Dead," *The New York Times*, August 27, 2005, p. A8.

5. Tim Collie, Madeline Baro Diaz, and Bill Hirschman, "South Florida Begins Picking up After Katrina's Sucker Punch," *Knight Ridder Tribune News Service*, August 26, 2005, p. 1.

6. Treaster, p. A8.

7. Mark Schleifstein, "Katrina Bulks Up to Become a Perfect Storm," *Times-Picayune*, August 28, 2005, p. 1.

8. John McQuaid and Mark Schleifstein, "The Big One; A Major Hurricane Could Decimate the Region, but Flooding From Even a Moderate Storm Could Kill Thousands. It's Just a Matter of Time," *Times-Picayune*, June 24, 2002, p. 1.

9. Ibid.

10. Neil Johnson, "Awaiting Disaster," *Tampa Tribune*, August 29, 2005, p. 1.

11. Joseph B. Treaster and Abby Goodnough, "Powerful Storm Threatens Havoc Along Gulf Coast," *The New York Times*, August 29, 2005, p. A1.

12. National Hurricane Center, "Hurricane Katrina Advisory #25," August 28, 2005, <http://www.nhc.noaa.gov/archive/2005/pub/al122005.public.025.shtml> (November 5, 2005).

Chapter 2. What Is a Hurricane?

1. Atlantic Oceanographic and Meteorological Laboratory of the National Oceanic Atmospheric Administration, "Saffir-

Simpson Hurricane Scale," November 5, 2005, <http://www. aoml.noaa.gov/general/lib/laescae.html> (November 5, 2005).

2. National Weather Service National Hurricane Center, "Hurricane Katrina Advisory #23," August 28, 2005, <http:// www.nhc.noaa.gov/archive/2005/pub/al122005.public. 023.shtml> (November 22, 2005).

3. Kerry Emanuel, *Divine Wind*, Oxford University Press, New York, 2005, pp. 54–61.

4. "The Saffir-Simpson Hurricane Scale," *National Hurricane Center*, September 19, 2003, <http://www.nhc. noaa.gov/aboutsshs.shtml> (February 25, 2005).

5. National Hurricane Center, "Hurricane Basics," June 30, 2005, <http://www.nhc.noaa.gov/HAW2/english/basics. shtml> (November 22, 2005).

6. Michael King, "MODIS Atmosphere," *NASA*, August 28, 2005, <http://modis-atmos.gsfc.nasa.gov/> (November 5, 2005).

7. National Weather Service National Hurricane Center, "Hurricane Katrina Advisory #25," August 28, 2005, <http:// www.nhc.noaa.gov/archive/2005/pub/al122005.public. 025.shtml> (November 5, 2005).

8. National Hurricane Center, "Have you seen the 'Weather Bullies?'" June 30, 2005, <http://www.nhc.noaa. gov/HAW2/english/kids.shtml> (November 5, 2005).

9. Ibid.

Chapter 3. Katrina Strikes

1. Jim Reed and Mike Theiss, "Storm Chasers Extreme Video Footage," *Today Show*, n.d., <http://video.msn.com/v/ us/v.htm?f=00&g=f91ef032-b8cc-446f-96b1-b04e4bd96ba1&t =m5&p=Source_Today%20Show> (November 5, 2005).

2. Thomas Korosec, "Katrina: The Aftermath: 'I've never seen anything like this': Gulfport, in the Line of Fire, Takes a Severe Beating," *Houston Chronicle*, August 30, 2005, p. 1.

3. Dahleen Glanton, "Biloxi Resident Emerges From Hiding to Find Her Town in Shambles," *Knight Ridder Tribune News Service*, August 30, 2005, p. 1.

4. Shaila Dewan, "In Coastal City, Ruin All Around," *New York Times*, August 30, 2005, p. A1.

5. Korosec, p. 1.

6. Scott Gold, Ellen Barry and Stephen Braun, "Katrina's Rising Toll," *Los Angeles Times*, August 31, 2005, p. A1.

7. Howard Witt, "Gulf Coast Swamped by Hurricane Katrina," *Knight Ridder Tribune News Service, Washington*, August 29, 2005, p. 1.

8. Glanton, p. 6.

9. "State by State Blows," *The Patriot Ledger*, August 30, 2005, p. 6.

10. Associated Press, "Hurricane Tears Holes in Superdome Roof," *Telegraph-Herald*, August 29, 2005, p. A1.

Chapter 4. New Orleans Floods

1. Scott Gold, "New Orleans Devastated As Levees Fail To Hold Katrina: The Day After," *Pittsburgh Post-Gazette*, August 31, 2005, p. A1.

2. Howard Witt, "New Orleans ravaged; 80 percent of city submerged after levees burst; FEMA warns 1 million people in 3 states will need shelter," *Chicago Tribune*, August 31, 2005, p. 1.

3. Frank Main, "'I heard people screaming'; Residents Tell of Sudden Flooding, Rescues, Looting," *Chicago Sun-Times*, August 31, 2005, p. 9.

4. Ibid.

5. Jamie Wilson and Julian Borger, "New Orleans Deluged as Katrina Batters Coast: Storm Troopers; Some Residents Who Chose to Stay Reported Stranded or Dead: Katrina Batters New Orleans," *The Guardian*, August 30, 2005, p. 1.

6. John DuPont, "Firefighter: 'I felt like I was in a war zone,'" *Advocate*, September 8, 2005, p. 1G.

7. Paul Salopek and Deborah Horan, "How Places Of Refuge Went To Hell; Over 5 Increasingly Horrific Days, the Evacuees at the Superdome and Convention Center Came to Feel Like Prisoners and Prey," *Chicago Tribune*, September 15, 2005, p. 1.

8. Scott Gold, "Katrina's Rising Toll; Trapped in an Arena of Suffering; 'We are like animals,' a Mother Says Inside the Louisiana Superdome, Where Hope and Supplies are Sparse," *Los Angeles Times*, September 1, 2005, p. A1.

9. Salopek and Horan, p. 1.

10. Gold, p. A1.

11. Paul McLeary, "Holding Authority to Account," *CJRDaily*, September 2, 2005, <http://www.cjrdaily.org/politics/holding_authority_to_account.php> (December 6, 2005).

12. "Racism, Resources Blamed for Bridge Incident." *CNN.com*, September 13, 2005, <http://www.cnn.com/2005/US/09/13/katrina.bridge/> (November 5, 2005).

13. Ellen Barry, Scott Gold, and Stephen Braun, "In Katrina's Aftermath: Chaos And Survival," *Los Angeles Times*, September 2, 2005, p. A1.

14. Allen G. Breed, "Ruined City In Anarchy," *St. Louis Post-Dispatch*, September 2, 2005, p. A1.

15. Brett Martel, "'Engineering nightmare': Water keeps rising in New Orleans," *Deseret News*, August 31, 2005, <http://deseretnews.com/dn/view/0,1249,600160022,00.html> (November 11, 2005).

16. Jim Ritter, "City's famed pumps too flooded to work; Getting them running again could take several days," *Chicago Sun-Times*, September 2, 2005, p. 13.

Chapter 5. After Katrina

1. Tatsha Robertson, "Evacuees Find Refuge In Houston Stadium," *Boston Globe*, September 2, 2005, p. A1.

2. Todd S. Purdum, "Across U.S., Outrage at Response," *New York Times*, September 3, 2005, p. A1.

3. Ibid.

4. Meet the Press, "Transcript for Sept. 4, 2005," MSNBC, September 2, 2005, <http://www.msnbc.msn.com/id/9179790/> (November 5, 2005).

5. John Christoffersen, "KATRINA'S AFTERMATH / Majority of the dead 61 or older / Study of victims ID'd so far

says many unwilling or unable to evacuate," *Houston Chronicle*, October 25, 2005, p. 9.

6. Ibid.

7. Doug Simpson "More may be arrested in deaths of patients," *Orlando Sentinel*, October 22, 2005, p. A21.

8. Robert Little, "Is It Safe for Big Easy Evacuees to Return?" *Orlando Sentinel*, September 19, 2005, p. A11.

9. Michael Graczyk, "Katrina Evacuees in Texas Must Now Flee Again," *St. Louis Post-Dispatch*, September 21, 2005, p. A7.

10. Tim Harper, "Motorists Trapped on Highways; Tempers Fray as Texans Heed Call to Evacuate Officials Caught Off Guard by Traffic Flow, Urge Calm," *Toronto Star*, September 23, 2005, p. A7.

11. Dwight Ott, Nicholas Spangler, and Gary Estwick, "Levee design meets with disasters High Water From Rita Surmounts Sections Repaired by Corps," *St. Louis Post-Dispatch*, September 25, 2005, p. B6.

Chapter 6. The Next Hurricane

1. "Post-Tropical Cyclone Report for Hurricane Katrina," *National Weather Service Forecasting Office*, November 9, 2005, <http://www.srh.noaa.gov/lix/html/psh_katrina.htm> (November 13, 2005).

2. Warren Vieth and Ricardo Alonso-Zaldivar, "Feds Mobilizing Response to Rita; Calm Projected: Bush, FEMA Prepare for Storm," *Seattle Times*, September 22, 2005, p. A18.

3. Ibid.

4. National Hurricane Center, "Disaster Supply Kit," *Hurricane Preparedness*, n.d., <http://www.nhc.noaa.gov/HAW2/english/prepare/supply_kit.shtml> (December 6, 2005).

5. Paul Salopek and Deborah Horan, "How Places Of Refuge Went To Hell; Over 5 Increasingly Horrific Days, the Evacuees at the Superdome and Convention Center Came to Feel Like Prisoners and Prey," *Chicago Tribune*, September 15, 2005, p. 1.

Glossary

barricade—A barrier that blocks a path.

breach—A break.

debacle—A disaster.

dropsonde—A canister filled with weather-sensing devices.

evacuate (evacuation, evacuee)—To leave an area because of danger.

eye—The center of a hurricane where winds are low and the sky is clear.

eye wall—The dense clouds that surround the eye of a hurricane.

generator—A machine that provides electricity.

global warming—A steady increase in the worlds overall temperature.

levee—An embankment (raised area) built to prevent flooding.

predict (prediction)—To make an educated guess as to what will happen in the future.

ration—To limit the amount of something so there is enough to around.

satellite—A device that orbits (travels around) the earth.

storm surge—Water that is pushed over the shoreline by strong winds.

sustained—When something is continued.

tropical storm—A rotating storm system formed in the tropics with winds of 39 mph to 73 mph.

wind shear—The difference in wind speed and/or direction at the surface compared to higher levels of altitude.

Books

CNN Staff. *Hurricane Katrina: CNN Reports: State of Emergency.* Kansas City: Andrews McMeel Publishing, 2005.

Editors of Time Magazine. *Hurricane Katrina.* New York: Time, Inc., Home Entertainment, 2005.

Hemphill, Barbara Booth. *A Wind From God: Prayers for Recovery From Hurricane Katrina.* Kingwood, Tex.: Shadow Verse Press, 2005.

Moyer, Susan M., ed. *Katrina: Stories of Rescue, Recovery and Rebuilding in the Eye of the Storm.* Champaign, Ill.: Spotlight Press, L.L.C., 2005.

Internet Addresses

Hurricane Preparedness for Kids

<http://www.nhc.noaa.gov/HAW2/english/kids.shtml>
Information designed for kids on the different hurricane threats with storm threat posters and an emergency kit scavenger hunt list.

Hurricane Strike!

<http://meted.ucar.edu/hurrican/strike/index.htm>
A multimedia approach to hurricane science and safety with interactive games, video, quizzes, and teacher information.

Tropical Twisters: Hurricanes How They Work
and What They Do

<http://kids.earth.nasa.gov/archive/hurricane/>
Information designed for kids on hurricanes including satellite images and information on hurricane hunters.